NOTICE:

This publication is intended to provide guidance and information to the trade community. It reflects the position on or interpretation of the applicable laws or regulations by U.S. Customs and Border Protection (CBP) as of the date of publication, which is shown on the front cover. It does not in any way replace or supersede those laws or regulations. Only the latest official version of the laws or regulations is authoritative.

Publication History

First Published: January 2009

PREFACE

On December 8, 1993, Title VI of the North American Free Trade Agreement Implementation Act (Pub. L. 103-182, 107 Stat. 2057), also known as the Customs Modernization or "Mod" Act, became effective. These provisions amended many sections of the Tariff Act of 1930 and related laws.

Two new concepts that emerge from the Mod Act are "***informed compliance***" and "***shared responsibility***," which are premised on the idea that in order to maximize voluntary compliance with laws and regulations of U.S. Customs and Border Protection, the trade community needs to be clearly and completely informed of its legal obligations. Accordingly, the Mod Act imposes a greater obligation on CBP to provide the public with improved information concerning the trade community's rights and responsibilities under customs regulations and related laws. In addition, both the trade and U.S. Customs and Border Protection share responsibility for carrying out these requirements. For example, under Section 484 of the Tariff Act, as amended (19 U.S.C. 1484), the importer of record is responsible for using reasonable care to enter, classify and determine the value of imported merchandise and to provide any other information necessary to enable U.S. Customs and Border Protection to properly assess duties, collect accurate statistics, and determine whether other applicable legal requirements, if any, have been met. CBP is then responsible for fixing the final classification and value of the merchandise. An importer of record's failure to exercise reasonable care could delay release of the merchandise and, in some cases, could result in the imposition of penalties.

Regulations and Rulings in CBP's Office of International Trade ("OT") has been given a major role in meeting the informed compliance responsibilities of U.S. Customs and Border Protection. In order to provide information to the public, CBP has issued a series of informed compliance publications on new or revised requirements, regulations or procedures, and a variety of classification and valuation issues.

This publication, prepared by the Border Security & Trade Compliance Division of Regulations and Rulings, is part of a series of informed compliance publications advising the public of new or revised regulations or procedures. "Coastwise Trade: Merchandise" is a guideline for the coastwise transportation of merchandise as it relates to the Jones Act. We sincerely hope that this material, together with seminars and increased access to rulings of U.S. Customs and Border Protection, will help the trade community to improve voluntary compliance with customs laws and to understand the relevant administrative processes.

The material in this publication is provided for general information purposes only. Because many complicated factors can be involved in customs issues, an importer may wish to obtain a ruling under Regulations of U.S. Customs and Border Protection, 19 C.F.R. Part 177, or to obtain advice from an expert who specializes in customs matters, for example, a licensed customs broker, attorney or consultant.

Comments and suggestions are welcomed and should be addressed to the Executive Director, Regulations and Rulings, Office of International Trade, U.S. Customs and Border Protection, 799 9th Street, NW, (Mint Annex), Washington, D.C. 20229.

Sandra L. Bell
Executive Director, Regulations and Rulings
Office of International Trade

(This page intentionally left blank)

(This page intentionally left blank)

(This page intentionally left blank)

(This page intentionally left blank)

INTRODUCTION

The purpose of this Informed Compliance Publication (ICP) is to identify the laws and regulations that are to be adhered to by the trade community engaged in the coastwise transportation of merchandise, such that the trade community is informed of its legal obligations, and in order to maximize voluntary compliance with laws and regulations enforced by U.S. Customs and Border Protection (CBP).

Under Title 19 of the Code of Federal Regulations § 4.80b (19 CFR § 4.80b), "[a] coastwise transportation of merchandise takes place, within the meaning of the coastwise laws, when merchandise laden at a point embraced within the coastwise laws ("coastwise point") is unladen at another coastwise point, regardless of the origin or ultimate destination of the merchandise." For example, a coastwise transportation occurs when merchandise is loaded onto a vessel in San Francisco and carried to Seattle, where it is unloaded.

Specifically, in this publication, CBP will summarize:

- The "Jones Act"

- CBP Regulations

- Exceptions

- Waivers

Background

For over 200 years, the United States Customs Service[1], now CBP, has been responsible for enforcing and administering laws and regulations[2] which set forth procedures to control and oversee vessels arriving in, and departing from, U.S. ports and the coastwise transportation of merchandise between U.S. ports.

Federal laws protecting U.S. shipping date back to the First Congress in 1789. American shipping in the United States coastwise[3] trade has been protected from foreign competition, in order to encourage the development of an American merchant marine, for both national defense and commercial purposes. As a result, all vessels

---

[1] The U.S. Customs Service was removed from the Treasury Department and became a component of the Department of Homeland Security (DHS), pursuant to the Homeland Security Act of 2002, Pub. L. 107-296 (November 25, 2002), secs. 403, 411, and is now known as U.S. Customs and Border Protection (CBP) (DHS Delegation Number 7010.1, of June 20, 2003).

[2] Customs (now CBP) has always enforced coastwise laws except for a 58-year period (1884-1942) when the responsibility resided with the former Bureau of Navigation under the Treasury and Commerce.

[3] In this context, the term "coastwise" refers to vessels engaged in domestic trade, or those traveling regularly from port to port in the United States. BLACK'S LAW DICTIONARY 233 (5th ed. 1979).

engaged in the coastwise trade have been required to be American-built and American-owned.

The coastwise law governing the transportation of merchandise was first established by Section 27 of the Merchant Marine Act of 1920, sponsored by Senator Wesley L. Jones (hence its name, the "Jones Act"), which revamped the U.S. shipping laws governing cabotage, shipping mortgages, seamen's personal injury claims, etc. That statute provided that "[N]o merchandise shall be transported by water, or by land and water, on penalty of forfeiture thereof, between points in the United States, including districts, territories, and possessions thereof embraced within the coastwise laws, either directly or via a foreign port, or for any part of the transportation, in any other vessel than a vessel built in and documented under the laws of the United States and owned by persons who are citizens of the United States."

As stated above, the intent of the coastwise laws, including the Jones Act, was to protect U.S. shipping interests. The coastwise laws are highly protectionist provisions that are intended to create a "coastwise monopoly" in order to protect and develop the American merchant marine, shipbuilding, etc. (see Headquarters Ruling (HQ) 116630 (March 27, 2006) and cases cited therein).

Coastwise Laws

Generally, the coastwise laws prohibit the transportation of passengers or merchandise between points in the United States embraced within the coastwise laws in any vessel other than a vessel built in, documented under the laws of, and owned by citizens of the United States.

Title 46 of the United States Code covers the coastwise laws, including the Jones Act, that are administered by CBP. Specifically, the Jones Act was formerly found in 46 U.S.C. App. 883. However, pursuant to Public Law 109-304, 120 Stat. 1632, enacted on October 6, 2006, Title 46, United States Code (U.S.C.), setting forth the shipping laws was substantially reorganized and recodified. Consequently, the Jones Act is now codified at 46 U.S.C. § 55102.

THE JONES ACT

Transportation of Merchandise—46 U.S.C. § 55102

The Jones Act (46 U.S.C. § 55102), provides that the transportation of merchandise between U.S. points is reserved for U.S.-built, owned, and documented vessels. Pursuant to section 55102, "a vessel may not provide any part of the transportation of merchandise by water, or by land and water, between points in the United States to which the coastwise laws apply, either directly or via a foreign port, unless the vessel— (1) is wholly owned by citizens of the United States for purposes of engaging in the coastwise trade; and (2) has been issued a certificate of documentation with a coastwise endorsement under chapter 121 of Title 46 or is exempt from documentation but would otherwise be eligible for such a certificate and endorsement."

Consequently, foreign-flag vessels are prohibited from engaging in the coastwise trade—transporting merchandise between U.S. coastwise points. In addition, the same prohibitions apply to U.S.-flag vessels that do not have a coastwise endorsement on their document, i.e., are not coastwise qualified.

What is Merchandise?

CBP uses the definitions provided in 46 U.S.C. § 55102(a) and 19 U.S.C. § 1401(c), to determine what is considered merchandise for purposes of enforcing the Jones Act.

Pursuant to 19 U.S.C. § 1401(c), the word "merchandise" means goods, wares and chattels of every description and includes merchandise the importation of which is prohibited. Monetary instruments as defined in section 5312 of Title 31 of the United States Code are also considered merchandise.

Statutory Definition: 46 U.S.C. § 55102(a) the term "merchandise," as used in 46 U.S.C. § 55102, is defined for the purpose of that statute as including 1) merchandise owned by the United States Government, a State, or a subdivision of a State; and 2) valueless material.

What is not Merchandise?

Equipment of the transporting vessel is not considered merchandise, nor is the baggage or personal effects of crew or passengers. Vessel equipment includes items which are "necessary and appropriate for the navigation, operation or maintenance of a vessel and for the comfort and safety of the persons on board." See Treasury Decision (T.D.) 49815(4) (1939).

Similarly, sea stores, i.e., supplies for the consumption, sustenance, and medical needs of the crew and passengers during the voyage are not considered merchandise. See T.D. 40934 (1925).

Accordingly, these items are not considered merchandise when they are transported in the vessel on which they are used.

Application of the Jones Act

1. Where Does the Jones Act Apply?

The Jones Act applies to the United States, including the island territories and possessions of the United States, e.g., Puerto Rico. See 46 U.S.C. § 55101(a). However, the coastwise laws generally do not apply to the following: 1) American

Samoa; 2) the Northern Mariana Islands; 3) Canton Island; or 4) the Virgin Islands. <u>See</u> 46 U.S.C. § 55101(b).

2.   <u>U.S. Territorial Waters</u>

The territorial waters of the United States consist of the territorial sea, defined as the belt, three nautical miles wide, seaward of the territorial sea baseline, and to points located in internal waters, landward of the territorial sea baseline, in cases where the baseline and coastline differ.   This includes all inland navigable waterways.   In interpreting the Jones Act, CBP has consistently ruled that a point in the United States territorial waters is a point in the United States embraced within the coastwise laws.

3.   <u>Outer Continental Shelf: Coastwise Points</u>

In order for an activity to constitute coastwise trade, there must be a transportation between "coastwise points." In addition to the U.S. territorial waters as defined above, coastwise points also include certain points on the Outer Continental Shelf (OCS):

Section 4(a) of the Outer Continental Shelf Lands Act of 1953, as amended (43 U.S.C. § 1333(a); "OSCLA"), provides in part that the laws of the United States are extended to: "the subsoil and seabed of the outer Continental Shelf and to all artificial islands, and all installations and other devices permanently or temporarily attached to the seabed, which may be erected thereon for the purpose of exploring for, developing, or producing resources therefrom…to the same extent as if the outer Continental Shelf were an area of exclusive Federal jurisdiction within a state."

Therefore, the Jones Act is extended to artificial islands and similar structures, as well as to mobile oil drilling rigs, drilling platforms, and other devices attached to the seabed of the outer continental shelf for the purpose of resource exploration operations. For example, drilling rigs located on the OCS are considered points or places in the U.S. for purposes of enforcing the Jones Act. Similarly, floating, anchored warehouse vessels, when anchored on the OCS to supply drilling rigs on the OCS, are also points in the U.S. for purposes of the Jones Act, since they are essential to the operation of the drilling rig. <u>See</u> Customs Service Decisions (C.S.D.s) 81-214 and 83-52; <u>see also</u>, HQ 107579 (May 9, 1985). Likewise, the Jones Act is extended to mobile oil drilling rigs during the period they are secured to or submerged onto the seabed of the OCS. <u>See</u> Treasury Decision (T.D.) 54281(1). The installation or device must be permanently or temporarily attached, and it must be used for the purpose of exploring for, developing or producing resources therefrom, in order to be considered a coastwise point.

Requirements: Coastwise-Qualified

1.   <u>Vessel Documentation</u>

The 11th Act of Congress in 1789 established the documentation system for U.S. vessels, in order to regulate coastwise trade. The United States Coast Guard (USCG) issues certificates of documentation, and determines the eligibility of vessels for a coastwise endorsement to appear on such certificates.

2.   Coastwise Endorsement

A vessel that is built in, documented under the laws of, and owned by citizens of the United States, and which obtains a coastwise endorsement from the USCG, is referred to as "coastwise-qualified." Specifically, the term "coastwise-qualified vessel" means a U.S.-flag vessel having a certificate of documentation with a coastwise endorsement under 46 U.S.C. § 12112.

3.   Vessel Eligibility

The certificates of documentation issued by the USCG provide conclusive evidence of nationality for international purposes, which allow qualified vessels to engage in the restricted coastwise trade. In order to engage in the coastwise trade, a vessel must meet certain eligibility requirements to qualify for a certificate of documentation and coastwise endorsement (e.g., build, ownership, etc.). These requirements are solely within the purview of the USCG. They make determinations such as what constitutes "U.S. build," for purposes of vessel eligibility for documentation and coastwise endorsement.

IMPLEMENTING REGULATIONS

Vessels entitled to engage in coastwise trade—19 CFR § 4.80

The applicable CBP regulations governing the Jones Act are found in Title 19 of the Code of Federal Regulations (CFR), Part 4 (19 CFR Part 4). These regulations closely track the statutory requirements for vessels engaging in coastwise trade.

In order for any vessel of five net tons or more to engage in coastwise transportation, it must have a coastwise endorsement on its certificate of documentation. Vessels of less than five net tons may not be documented by the USCG. For those vessels to engage in coastwise transportation, they must, except for their tonnage, otherwise be entitled to be documented with a coastwise endorsement. See 19 CFR § 4.80(a)(2).

Coastwise transportation of merchandise—19 CFR § 4.80b

Under 19 CFR § 4.80b, "[a] coastwise transportation of merchandise takes place, within the meaning of the coastwise laws, when merchandise laden at a point embraced within the coastwise laws ("coastwise point") is unladen at another coastwise point, regardless of the origin or ultimate destination of the merchandise." For example, a coastwise transportation occurs when merchandise is loaded onto a vessel in San Francisco and carried to Seattle, where it is unloaded.

New and Different Product—19 CFR § 4.80b(a)

Under the CBP regulations, merchandise is not considered to be transported coastwise if at an intermediate port or place other than a coastwise point (e.g., foreign port or place or at a port or place in a territory or possession of the U.S. not subject to the coastwise laws), it is manufactured or processed into a "new and different product." The subsequent transportation of the new and different product to a coastwise point would not be deemed a violation of the coastwise laws. See HQ 116650 (June 9, 2006) (processing fuel oil in Canada into conventional gasoline resulted in manufacture or processing into new and different products).

Prematurely landed merchandise—19 CFR § 4.34

CBP regulations provide a very narrow exception to the coastwise merchandise statute for merchandise that is prematurely discharged. Specifically, under 19 CFR § 4.34(a), inward foreign cargo that is "prematurely landed and left behind" by an importing vessel "through error or emergency" may be reladen on the next available vessel owned or chartered by the owner of the importing vessel for transportation to the originally intended destination, provided that the importing vessel "actually entered" the port of destination of the prematurely landed cargo. In effect under these circumstances, the merchandise could be reladen on a non-coastwise-qualified vessel and transported to the intended destination. See HQ H006047 (February 2, 2007) (citing Customs Bureau Letter of December 28, 1956, MA 192018.4, to Collector, Tampa, FL). However, the terms and conditions of § 4.34(a) are strictly construed, such that the error or emergency must pertain to the cargo itself, rather than to the vessel (see HQ H006047 and cases cited therein).

Empty Cargo Containers, Stevedoring Equipment—19 CFR § 4.93

CBP regulations allow U.S. vessels that do not have a coastwise endorsement, as well as foreign-flag vessels of nations that grant reciprocal privileges to vessels of the U.S., to transport certain articles between points embraced within the coastwise laws of the United States. These items include empty cargo vans, empty lift vans, and empty shipping tanks and the equipment for use with said empty cargo vans, lift vans and shipping tanks; empty barges specifically designed to be carried aboard a vessel and equipment (excluding propulsion equipment) for use with such barges; and empty instruments of international traffic (IIT). These items are exempt from the application of CBP regulations concerning the coastwise laws, if they are owned or leased by the owner or operator of the transporting vessel and are transported for his use in handling the cargo in foreign trade. Similarly, stevedoring equipment and material are also exempt, if they are owned or leased by the owner or operator of the transporting vessel, or owned or leased by the stevedoring company contracting for the lading or unlading of that vessel, and is transported without charge for use in the handling of cargo in foreign trade. The list of nations that extend reciprocal privileges to U.S. vessels is set forth at 19 CFR § 4.93(b).

PENALTY

The statute, 46 U.S.C. § 55102(c), provides in pertinent part that merchandise transported in violation of the Jones Act "is liable to seizure by and forfeiture to the Government. Alternatively, an amount equal to the value of the merchandise (as determined by the Secretary of [the Department of] Homeland Security or the actual cost of the transportation, whichever is greater, may be recovered from any person transporting the merchandise or causing the merchandise to be transported."

The applicable CBP regulations regarding penalties for violating coastwise laws are found in 19 CFR § 4.80(b), which provide for forfeiture of the merchandise or, in the discretion of the port director, forfeiture of a monetary amount up to the value of the merchandise. However, CBP may remit without payment any penalty which arises for violation of the coastwise laws if there is satisfactory evidence that the violation occurred as a direct result of an arrival of the transporting vessel in distress. See 19 CFR § 171.11(c); see also mitigation guidelines set forth in ICP entitled "Mitigation Guidelines: Fines, Penalties, Forfeitures and Liquidated Damages," February 2004 revision, p. 183 *et seq*.

EXCEPTIONS

Former 46 U.S.C. App. 883 contained a number of "provisos" or exceptions to the Jones Act. In the recodification of Title 46, the provisos were codified into separate sections, as summarized below:

Transportation of hazardous waste—Sec. 55105(b):
Although the transportation of hazardous waste is deemed to be transportation of merchandise under section 55102, under specified circumstances, the prohibition does not apply to certain foreign vessels.

Merchandise transferred between barges—Sec. 55106:
Under specified circumstances, merchandise may be transferred between barges if reciprocal privileges are extended to U.S. vessels.

Empty cargo containers and barges—Sec. 55107:
In general, section 55102 does not apply to the transportation of empty cargo vans, empty lift vans, or empty shipping tanks; equipment for use with cargo vans, lift vans, or shipping tanks; empty barges specifically designed for carriage aboard a vessel and equipment (except propulsion equipment) for use with those barges; empty instruments for international traffic (IIT); stevedoring equipment and material, if the government of the nation of the vessel's registry extends reciprocal privileges to vessels of the United States[4].

---

[4] The list of nations is found at 19 CFR § 4.93.

Platform jackets—Sec. 55108:
Section 55108(b) authorizes the transportation of certain "platform jackets."

Use of foreign documented oil spill response vessels—Sec. 55113:
An oil spill response vessel documented under the laws of a foreign country may operate in waters of the United States on an emergency basis, for the purpose of recovering, transporting, and unloading in a U.S. port oil discharged as a result of an oil spill in or near those waters, if an adequate number and type of U.S. coastwise-qualified oil spill response vessels are unavailable and the foreign country extends reciprocal privileges to U.S. vessels.

Canadian rail lines—Sec. 55116:
Section 55102 does not apply to the transportation of merchandise between points in the continental United States, including Alaska, over through routes in part over Canadian rail lines and connecting water facilities if the routes are recognized by the Surface Transportation Board and rate tariffs for the routes have been filed with the Board.

Great Lakes rail route—Sec. 55117:
Section 55102 generally does not apply to the transportation of merchandise loaded on a railroad car when the railroad car is transported in a railroad car ferry operating between fixed terminals on the Great Lakes as part of a rail route under certain circumstances.

Yukon River—Sec. 55119:
Section 55102 currently does not apply to the transportation of merchandise on the Yukon River, until the Alaska Railroad is completed.

Transportation of merchandise and passengers on Canadian vessels—Sec. 55121:
Section 55121(b)(2) provides that the prohibitions of section 55102 currently do not apply to the transportation of merchandise on Canadian vessels between Hyder, Alaska, and other points in southeastern Alaska or in the U.S. outside Alaska, until the Secretary of Transportation determines that service by vessels of the U.S. is available to provide such transportation.

WAIVER AUTHORITY—46 U.S.C. § 501

National Defense

The Jones Act can only be waived in the interest of national defense, pursuant to 46 U.S.C. § 501. Under 46 U.S.C. § 501, the Secretary of Defense may request the Secretary of the Department of Homeland Security (DHS) to waive the Jones Act to the extent the Secretary of Defense considers such a waiver necessary in the interest of national defense. In this instance, CBP, pursuant to a delegation of authority from the Secretary of DHS shall grant the waiver. For all other waiver requests, the Secretary of DHS is authorized to grant the waiver request if the Secretary of DHS considers it necessary in the interest of national defense (46 U.S.C. § 501(b)). It should be noted that in this latter instance, P.L. 110-417, section 3510, (122 Stat. 4356, enacted on October 14, 2008), amended § 501(b), to require that the Maritime Administrator be consulted regarding the non-availability of qualified United States flag capacity to meet national defense requirements, before the Secretary of DHS grants the waiver request.

Waiver Request

A waiver request should include the purpose for which waiver is sought, port(s) involved, and estimated period of time for which the waiver is sought.

Requests to waive the provisions of the coastwise laws administered by CBP should be referred to the Cargo Security, Carriers & Immigration Branch, Regulations and Rulings, Office of International Trade, U.S. Customs and Border Protection, 799 9th Street, NW, Washington, DC 20229, phone (202) 325-0030, fax (202) 325-0152.

Coordination with Other Agencies

CBP's enforcement and administration of the Jones Act requires coordination with other interested agencies, such as the Maritime Administration of the U.S. Department of Transportation, the U.S. Coast Guard, the U.S. Department of Defense, and the U.S. Department of Energy. As mentioned above, the USCG determines vessel eligibility for coastwise endorsement and issues certificates of documentation. The U.S. Department of Transportation's Maritime Administration monitors and assesses the operating status of U.S.-flag vessels, and advises CBP on such U.S. vessel availability. The U.S. Department of Energy monitors energy supply needs and advises CBP during periods of actual or imminent shortages of energy on requests for waivers of the Jones Act. Similarly, the U.S. Department of Defense ascertains the impact of certain energy supply situations on its operations, and whether a waiver request is in the interest of national defense. If the Department of Defense is the requesting party for a waiver, CBP grants the waiver request. For all other requests, CBP makes a recommendation to the Secretary of DHS who is the deciding authority on the waiver request.

ADDITIONAL INFORMATION

The Internet

The home page of U.S. Customs and Border Protection on the Internet's World Wide Web, provides the trade community with current, relevant information regarding CBP operations and items of special interest. The site posts information -- which includes proposed regulations, news releases, publications and notices, etc. -- that can be searched, read on-line, printed or downloaded to your personal computer. The web site was established as a trade-friendly mechanism to assist the importing and exporting community. The web site also links to the home pages of many other agencies whose importing or exporting regulations that U.S. Customs and Border Protection helps to enforce. The web site also contains a wealth of information of interest to a broader public than the trade community. For instance, on June 20, 2001, CBP launched the "Know Before You Go" publication and traveler awareness campaign designed to help educate international travelers.

The web address of U.S. Customs and Border Protection is http://www.cbp.gov

Customs Regulations

The current edition of *Customs Regulations of the United States* is a loose-leaf, subscription publication available from the Superintendent of Documents, U.S. Government Printing Office, Washington, DC 20402; telephone (202) 512-1800. The latest edition of Title 19, *Code of Federal Regulations*, is also available for sale from the same address. All proposed and final regulations are published in the *Federal Register*, which is published daily by the Office of the Federal Register, National Archives and Records Administration, and distributed by the Superintendent of Documents. Information about on-line access to the *Federal Register* may be obtained by calling (202) 512-1530 between 7 a.m. and 5 p.m. Eastern time. These notices are also published in the weekly *Customs Bulletin* described below.

Customs Bulletin

The *Customs Bulletin and Decisions ("Customs Bulletin")* is a weekly publication that contains decisions, rulings, regulatory proposals, notices and other information of interest to the trade community. It also contains decisions issued by the U.S. Court of International Trade. Each year, the Government Printing Office publishes bound volumes of the *Customs Bulletin*. Subscriptions may be purchased from the Superintendent of Documents at the address and phone number listed above.

Importing Into the United States

This publication provides an overview of the importing process and contains general information about import requirements. The current edition of *Importing Into the United States* contains much new and revised material brought about pursuant to the Customs Modernization Act ("Mod Act"). The Mod Act has fundamentally altered the relationship between importers and U.S. Customs and Border Protection by shifting to the importer the legal responsibility for declaring the value, classification, and rate of duty applicable to entered merchandise.

The current edition contains a section entitled "Informed Compliance." A key component of informed compliance is the shared responsibility between U.S. Customs and Border Protection and the import community, wherein CBP communicates its requirements to the importer, and the importer, in turn, uses reasonable care to assure that CBP is provided accurate and timely data pertaining to his or her importation.

Single copies may be obtained from local offices of U.S. Customs and Border Protection, or from the Office of Public Affairs, U.S. Customs and Border Protection, 1300 Pennsylvania Avenue NW, Washington, DC 20229. An on-line version is available at the CBP web site. *Importing Into the United States* is also available for sale, in single copies or bulk orders, from the Superintendent of Documents by calling (202) 512-1800, or by mail from the Superintendent of Documents, Government Printing Office, P.O. Box 371954, Pittsburgh, PA 15250-7054.

Informed Compliance Publications

U.S. Customs and Border Protection has prepared a number of Informed Compliance publications in the "*What Every Member of the Trade Community Should Know About:…*" series. Check the Internet web site http://www.cbp.gov for current publications.

Value Publications

Customs Valuation under the Trade Agreements Act of 1979 is a 96-page book containing a detailed narrative description of the customs valuation system, the customs valuation title of the Trade Agreements Act (§402 of the Tariff Act of 1930, as amended by the Trade Agreements Act of 1979 (19 U.S.C. §1401a)), the Statement of Administrative Action which was sent to the U.S. Congress in conjunction with the TAA, regulations (19 C.F.R. §§152.000-152.108) implementing the valuation system (a few sections of the regulations have been amended subsequent to the publication of the book) and questions and answers concerning the valuation system. A copy may be obtained from U.S. Customs and Border Protection, Office of International Trade, Regulations and Rulings, Valuation & Special Programs Branch, 799 9th Street, NW, (Mint Annex), Washington, D.C. 20229.

Customs Valuation Encyclopedia (with updates) is comprised of relevant statutory provisions, CBP Regulations implementing the statute, portions of the Customs Valuation Code, judicial precedent, and administrative rulings involving application of valuation law. A copy may be purchased for a nominal charge from the Superintendent of Documents, Government Printing Office, P.O. Box 371954, Pittsburgh, PA 15250-7054. This publication is also available on the Internet web site of U.S. Customs and Border Protection.

The information provided in this publication is for general information purposes only. Recognizing that many complicated factors may be involved in customs issues, an importer may wish to obtain a ruling under CBP Regulations, 19 C.F.R. Part 177, or obtain advice from an expert (such as a licensed Customs Broker, attorney or consultant) who specializes in customs matters. Reliance solely on the general information in this pamphlet may not be considered reasonable care.

Additional information may also be obtained from U.S. Customs and Border Protection ports of entry. Please consult your telephone directory for an office near you. The listing will be found under U.S. Government, Department of Homeland Security.

"Your Comments are Important"

The Small Business and Regulatory Enforcement Ombudsman and 10 regional Fairness Boards were established to receive comments from small businesses about Federal agency enforcement activities and rate each agency's responsiveness to small business. If you wish to comment on the enforcement actions of U.S. Customs and Border Protection, call 1-888-REG-FAIR (1-888-734-3247).

REPORT SMUGGLING 1-800-BE-ALERT

Visit our Internet web site: http://www.cbp.gov

www.ingramcontent.com/pod-product-compliance
Lightning Source LLC
Chambersburg PA
CBHW080646190526
45169CB00009B/3527